IT'S TIME TO LEARN ABOUT ANACONDAS

It's Time to Learn about ANACONDAS

Walter the Educator

Silent King Books
A WhichHead Entertainment Imprint

Copyright © 2025 by Walter the Educator

All rights reserved. No part of this book may be reproduced in any manner whatsoever without written per- mission except in the case of brief quotations embodied in critical articles and reviews.

First Printing, 2024

Disclaimer

This book is a literary work; the story is not about specific persons, locations, situations, and/or circumstances unless mentioned in a historical context. Any resemblance to real persons, locations, situations, and/or circumstances is coincidental. This book is for entertainment and informational purposes only. The author and publisher offer this information without warranties expressed or implied. No matter the grounds, neither the author nor the publisher will be accountable for any losses, injuries, or other damages caused by the reader's use of this book. The use of this book acknowledges an understanding and acceptance of this disclaimer.

It's Time to Learn about ANACONDAS is a collectible early learning book by Walter the Educator suitable for all ages belonging to Walter the Educator's Time to Eat Book Series. Collect more books at WaltertheEducator.com

USE THE EXTRA SPACE TO TAKE NOTES AND DOCUMENT YOUR MEMORIES

ANACONDAS

Deep in rivers, dark and wide,

It's Time to Learn about

Anacondas

Anacondas love to hide.

Slithering through the swampy ground,

This giant snake is all around!

It has no legs, it has no feet,

Yet it moves so smooth and neat.

With muscles strong, it slides with grace,

Through water fast, it loves to race!

Anacondas grow so long,

Big and heavy, thick and strong.

The biggest snake you'll ever see,

As long as five grown men, or three!

Its skin is green with spots so round,

Helping it hide without a sound.

It blends in well, so it can stay,

Waiting for its sneaky prey.

It's Time to Learn about
Anacondas

No sharp teeth to chew its food,

It swallows whole, that's what it'll do!

It wraps around, then holds on tight,

And squeezes with a mighty might!

It eats big meals, but not too fast,

One snack for months, that's how they last!

From fish to deer, and birds so high,

It catches food that passes by.

In water deep, it loves to play,

Gliding softly through the bay.

It holds its breath and dives down low,

Much like a fish, but off it'll go!

Baby snakes are born alive,

And from the start, they move and thrive.

No need for help, they slither free,

It's Time to Learn about

Anacondas

Into the jungle wild and free!

Though big and strong, it hides away,

It won't chase you, it's not that way.

It likes to rest and swim with ease,

Deep in rivers, under trees.

Now you know this giant snake,

A jungle swimmer in the lake.

The anaconda, big and long,

It's Time to Learn about

Anacondas

So strong and silent, yet so strong!

ABOUT THE CREATOR

Walter the Educator is one of the pseudonyms for Walter Anderson. Formally educated in Chemistry, Business, and Education, he is an educator, an author, a diverse entrepreneur, and he is the son of a disabled war veteran. "Walter the Educator" shares his time between educating and creating. He holds interests and owns several creative projects that entertain, enlighten, enhance, and educate, hoping to inspire and motivate you. Follow, find new works, and stay up to date with Walter the Educator™ at WaltertheEducator.com

www.ingramcontent.com/pod-product-compliance
Lightning Source LLC
LaVergne TN
LVHW052016060526
838201LV00059B/4058